MW01294450

Homemade and Skin Care Beauty Products

Easy to Make Lotions, Creams, Scrubs, Body Butters, Hair Products, Lip Care Recipes for Women and Men

Josephine Simon

Copyrights

Disclaimer and Terms of Use

Effort has been made to ensure that the information in this book is accurate and complete. However, the author and the publisher do not warrant the accuracy of the information, text, and graphics contained within the book due to the rapidly changing nature of science, research, known and unknown facts, and internet. The author and the publisher do not hold any responsibility for errors, omissions, or contrary interpretation of the subject matter herein. This book is presented solely for motivational and informational purposes only. The publisher and author of this book does not control or direct users' actions and are not responsible for the information or content shared, harm and/or action of the book readers. The presentation of the information is without contract or any type of guarantee assurance. This book is not meant to be used, nor should it be used, to diagnose or treat any medical condition. For diagnosis or treatment of any medical problem, consult your own physician. The publisher and author are not responsible for any specific health or allergy needs that may require medical supervision and are not liable for any damages or negative consequences from any treatment, action, application or preparation, to any person reading or following the information in this book. References, if any, are provided for informational purposes only and do not constitute endorsement of any websites or other sources. Readers should be aware that the websites listed in this book, if any, may change.

ISBN: 978-1542540551

Printed in the United States

MAPLEWOOD
– PUBLISHING –

Contents

Introduction

The skin is the largest organ of the human body, but it often doesn't get the attention it deserves. It is time to change that, because this very fact could be sucking some serious joy out of your life.

Here's why.

What's the first thing people see when they look at you? Your skin. Sure, other things like your beautiful eyes and pouty lips matter too, but not so much if they are surrounded by dry, crackly skin. No one wants to be *that* guy or girl, who people avoid getting too close to for fear of accidentally touching sandpaper skin. Moreover, it feels good to have soft and luscious skin. And as you age, your investment pays off, as skin that has been properly cared for will look much younger and healthier.

This is where a good skincare regime is necessary. You need to be nourishing your body from not only within, but also from the outside. A good skincare plan requires a variety of things, including ways to cleanse the skin to get rid of dead skin cells, and hydrating the skin so it remains supple and soft.

There are thousands of retail skincare products on the market. However, many of them contain harmful chemicals that might not be doing what you think they're doing – they might actually be hurting your skin. Remember that whatever you place on your skin seeps quickly into your body, so when you slather on a tube of something containing ingredients with long names you can't pronounce, you are probably absorbing these chemicals into your body.

The very best way to ensure that you are getting clean, natural, wholesome ingredients in your skincare products is to go with all-natural, organic products. Store-bought products can cost you a pretty penny. However, there's another way. The amazingly simple, supremely cost-effective, and all-natural alternative is to make your beauty products at home.

That may sound daunting, but once you start doing it, you'll be amazed at how simple it truly is. You'll wonder why you didn't start concocting your own products a long time ago.

In this book, you will find directions and recipes for very important components of your skincare and beauty regimen: body scrubs, body lotions, body butters, face creams, lip care, hair care, and even men's care.

You need to exfoliate to get rid of dead skin cells to reveal the beautifully young and pliable ones underneath. This is where scrubs come in. The recipes included in this book will have you feeling refreshed, rejuvenated, and tingly all over with lovely concoctions like Mint Chocolate Scrub and our special Epsom Foot Scrub.

Retaining moisture in your skin is the ultimate necessity to younger looking skin, and that's where body lotions and body butters come in. These two help you to pull moisture from the air and get it into your skin, as well as retain that moisture by creating a shield over the skin. We've combined the best of butters, oils, and essential oils to create all-natural and balanced moisturizing for the skin with concoctions like Double Chocolate Lotion and Strawberry Vanilla Butter.

The face is the first thing people notice, and it is also the most beaten and battered by the elements. Gentle, light, and soothing (yet highly effective) face creams like Apricot Moisture Cream can keep facial skin soft and hydrated. Other face creams can cleanse, protect and keep skin wrinkle-free. Your own homemade acne cream with grapeseed oil can keep your skin free of pimples.

The lips should not be neglected as this is where our skin is thinnest and most delicate. You need natural products that will keep your lips protected, conditioned, and their natural beauty enhanced. Try the luscious concoctions like Honey-Coconut Healing Balm or Cinnamon Spice Lip Plumper.

The chemicals that we put on our hair will also wreak havoc through the skin of the scalp. The Honey-Banana Hair Mask and Green Tea Shampoo use gentle ingredients from nature for beautiful hair and a healthy scalp.

Men are now more aware of the need to keep themselves well groomed using natural, healthful products. They can pamper themselves with concoctions made especially for men, such as the Lemony Foaming Facial Wash, or the Cool-As-A-Cucumber Windburn Balm.

The fact of the matter is that the better the ingredients you put on your body, the better job your skin can do to protect you. This will be reflected in the way it glows, in its plumpness, and how soft it feels to the touch. This is the one thing you can easily do right away to help you look better, feel better, and walk with the confidence of a beautiful person on the inside and out.

Body Scrubs

The idea of exfoliating the skin so it appears fresh and feels soft and supple can be traced back to one of the oldest medical documents in the world. The Ebers Papyrus is an ancient Egyptian scroll that details medical knowledge relating to everything from depression to how fluids are circulated in the body. It also sheds a light on the ancient Egyptian treatments for skin.

This circa 1500 BC scroll also relays some of the Egyptian secrets for gorgeous skin, including creating scrubs out of natural ingredients. Clearly, there is strong reason to believe that the simple concept of using some sort of abrasive natural materials to rid the skin of dead cells really does work and is an important part of any skincare regimen.

Benefits

Giving yourself a good scrub is akin to scraping off all the old, crusted bits from the bottom of a pot. Sure, at one time that skin you're holding on to was fresh and new, but it's seen its heyday! Now it forms a subtle layer over your body, dulling your natural brightness. When you slough it off, you're going to reveal a lovely new, soft layer underneath!

Getting rid of the old layer also means you're detoxifying the skin. In turn, your complexion glows. The sloughing off of the dead skin means fine lines disappear as the rough outer layer is eliminated. This elimination of the outer layer also has the added benefit of giving your skin a nice, clean appearance.

Cleaning the skin with a scrub also reduces oils and helps in preventing acne.

What You Need

Scrubs are supremely easy to make at home! You need very few ingredients, which are probably already in your kitchen!

Exfoliant Ingredients
Sugar
Salt
Coffee grinds
Rice (coarsely ground)
Nuts (ground)
Lentils (coarsely ground)

Moisturizing Ingredients
Extra virgin olive oil
Coconut oil
Coconut butter
Milk
Honey
Organic Ghee

Optional Ingredients
Essential oils (any that suit you)

Storage

Use an airtight jar to store your scrub. Generally, Mason jars work great. You can package the scrub in small jars to avoid exposing your whole batch to the air each time you go to use one.

What to Watch out For

Remember to do a small patch test on your skin before using the scrub all over your body, to ensure you are not allergic to any of the ingredients.

Body Scrub Recipes

Your Go-To Basic Scrub

This easy-to-recreate basic scrub includes ingredients you are likely to have in your kitchen. If you don't stock white sugar, you can substitute brown. Sugar is very beneficial when applied to the skin for a variety of reasons. One of the biggest are the alpha hydroxy acids (AHAs) that it contains. This is the good stuff that is going to reduce those wrinkles and create a nice even tone!

Makes: 18 ounces

Ingredients
1 ½ cups organic cane sugar
¾ cup extra virgin olive oil
1 teaspoon vanilla extract

Directions
1. Combine the ingredients in an airtight jar, mix well, and store in a cool place.
2. Moisten the skin and scrub with the mixture, wash off.

Green Tea Scrub

Green tea oil provides numerous benefits to the skin. It has been used for everything from treating itching to a light form of UV protection. Its amazing antioxidant qualities make it an age-defying powerhouse. This green tea scrub provides just the right amount of anti-aging oil to green tea balance.

Makes: 18 ounces

Ingredients
1 ½ cups organic cane sugar
¾ cup coconut oil
1 tablespoon green tea essential oil
1 teaspoon tea tree oil

Directions
1. Combine the ingredients in an airtight jar, mix well, and store in a cool place.
2. Moisten the skin and scrub with the mixture, wash off.

Chocolate Scrub

Cocoa not only smells divine, but it is also fantastic for the skin. Chocolate masks and baths have become popular due to cocoa's inherent antioxidant capabilities. When applied to the skin, these help to rid the body of skin-damaging free radicals.

Makes: 16 ounces

Ingredients
3 tablespoons organic cocoa powder
1 teaspoon cocoa essential oil
1 ¼ cups organic cane sugar
¾ cup coconut oil

Directions
1. Combine the ingredients in an airtight jar, mix well, and store in a cool place.
2. Moisten the skin and scrub with the mixture, wash off.

Coffee Scrub

Now you can have your coffee and drink it too, with this wonderfully aromatic coffee scrub made out of coffee grounds! The coffee grounds stimulate the skin. It's also believed that rubbing the grounds on cellulite helps to reduce it!

Makes: 12 ounces

Ingredients
½ cup coffee grounds
1 cup coconut oil
1 teaspoon vanilla extract

Directions
1. Combine the ingredients in an airtight jar, mix well, and store in a cool place.
2. Moisten the skin and scrub with the mixture, wash off.

Lemon Scrub

Drop a little lemon into your scrub, and you'll see it do amazing things for your skin – like magic. Rub the lemony scrub onto your elbows and knees and watch the dark spots disappear! Additionally, lemon's astringent properties help to truly clean the skin and make it brighter.

Makes: 12 ounces

Ingredients
2 teaspoons lemon peel, grated
1 tablespoon lemon juice
1 cup organic cane sugar
2 teaspoons vitamin E oil
½ cup coconut oil

Directions
1. Combine the ingredients in an airtight jar, mix well, and store in a cool place.
2. Moisten the skin and scrub with the mixture, wash off.

Mint Chocolate Scrub

Scrub this on your body in the morning, and be prepared to have the wheels in your head turning at ultimate speeds all day! The scent of peppermint has a big, positive affect on mental function in ways such as improving memory and focus.

Makes: 12 ounces

Ingredients
1 cup organic cane sugar
½ cup almond oil
2 tablespoons pure cocoa powder
1 teaspoon peppermint essential oil

Directions
1. Combine the ingredients in an airtight jar, mix well, and store in a cool place.
2. Moisten the skin and scrub with the mixture, wash off.

Epsom Foot Scrub

Dry, hardened spots on the skin are terrible to touch and pretty horrible to look at. They can be disheartening personally and quite embarrassing. This is why you must absolutely use this scrub to make your feet beautiful and lovely. Epsom salt is anti-fungal and helps to deodorize feet. In addition, the minerals also help to alleviate pain and discomfort. Your feet work hard for you, so it is definitely time to show them some love.

Makes: 12 ounces

Ingredients
¾ cup Epsom salt
¼ cup sea salt
½ cup coconut oil

Directions
1. Combine the ingredients in an airtight jar, mix well, and store in a cool place.
2. Moisten the skin and scrub with the mixture, wash off.

Rice and Honey Whitening Body Scrub

Rice powder has excellent exfoliating properties, and it also helps in brightening skin tone. Honey is one of the best organic applications for your skin. It works as an antibacterial and anti-aging product. It opens up the pores and it is a good natural moisturizer that soothes your skin. It makes your skin glow, and makes it soft and supple to touch.

Makes: 12 ounces

Ingredients
1 cup rice, coarsely ground
3 tablespoons honey
10-12 drops almond oil (use only for dry skin)

Directions
1. Combine the ingredients in an airtight jar, mix well, and store in a cool place.
2. Moisten the skin and scrub with the mixture for a couple of minutes, then wash it off.

Summer Red Lentil Body Scrub

Rose water helps you feel refreshed during summertime. It provides relief for itchiness or a burning sensation. Honey is a good moisturizer, an antioxidant, and an antibacterial too. It suits all types of skin and makes your skin supple. The red lentils help remove dead skin cells from your skin and also give to add a healthy glow.

Makes: 12 ounces

Ingredients
½ cup red lentils, coarsely ground
3 tablespoons honey
2 tablespoons rose water

Directions
1. Combine ingredients in an airtight jar, mix well and store in a cool place.
2. Moisten skin and scrub with mixture, wash off.

Red Lentil Body Scrub for Winter

Winter can rob your skin of its natural moisture. If you have dry skin, then moisturizing frequently is important. That is where organic ghee comes to the rescue – a heavy duty natural skin moisturizer. It works wonders on dry skin, making it soft and supple. The red lentils help remove dead skin cells and also give you a healthy glow.

Makes: 12 ounces

Ingredients
1 cup red lentils, coarsely ground
½ cup ghee
Rose essential oil (since ghee can have a strong aroma)

Directions
1. Combine the ingredients in an airtight jar, mix well, and store in a cool place.
2. Moisten the skin and scrub with the mixture, wash off.

Glowing Soft Skin Body Scrub

This body scrub is full of goodness. Aloe Vera works wonders for moisturizing your skin, and it works very well on dry skin in particular. It is a good skin conditioner and is rich in vitamin E. It also nourishes your skin and helps prevent wrinkles. Walnuts are loaded with vitamins and minerals that are great for the skin, and almonds are good source of vitamin E, which prevents wrinkles and gives a healthy glow to your skin. Honey is a great moisturizer for all types of skin.

Makes: 6 ounces
Preparation time: 5 minutes

Ingredients
1 leaf of aloe vera
2 walnuts, in the shell
2 almonds, in the shell
2 tablespoons honey

Directions
1. Remove the pulp from the aloe vera leaf.
2. Grind all the ingredients together to get a coarse paste.
3. Apply the mixture to the skin, and leave it on for 5 minutes. Scrub lightly in circular motions.
4. Wash it off with lukewarm water.
5. Always make the scrub fresh and use. Discard leftovers. Use it once a week for soft and supple skin.

Face Whitening Scrub for Dry Skin

Milk is a natural skin moisturizer, and it's great for dry skin. People with oily skin should avoid this scrub, as it will make your face oilier. Rice powder helps in getting rid of dead skin cells and is also known to whiten your skin tone. This scrub is best used at night.

Makes: 12 ounces

Ingredients
½ cup rice, coarsely powdered
½ cup lukewarm milk

Directions
1. Mix the rice powder and milk together in a bowl to form a paste.
2. Before bed, apply it on the face and scrub in a circular motion.
3. Wash it off with lukewarm water. Your face may feel a bit oily for the time being, but the natural oils from the milk will be absorbed into your skin, and you will be left with a fresh and dewy face the next morning.

Lemon Lavender Body Scrub

Scrubs are not just for getting rid of dead skin cells. Body scrubs are also known to help relieve tension and help the body relax. Epsom salt, when used in a scrub, relaxes your muscles and also helps reduce inflammation. Olive oil keeps the skin moist. Lemon juice acts as a bleaching agent, while the lavender helps you relax your senses. Used all together, this relaxing body scrub is just what you need for both body and mind after a tough day.

Makes: 12 ounces

Ingredients
1 ¼ cups Epsom salt or coarse salt crystals
¼ cup olive oil
¼ cup lemon juice
10 drops lavender essential oil

Directions
1. Combine the ingredients in an airtight jar, mix well, and store in a cool place.
2. Moisten the skin and scrub with the mixture, wash off.

Anti-inflammatory Body Scrub

Turmeric has anti-inflammatory and antibacterial properties that soothe your skin and help fight skin bacteria. Essential oils (depending on the type you choose) have their own skincare and relaxation benefits. Sugar and salt will help get rid of dead skin cells.

Makes: 25 ounces

Ingredients:
1 ½ cups salt
1 ½ cups sugar
3 tablespoons turmeric powder
6-8 drops essential oil of your choice

Directions
1. Combine the ingredients in an airtight jar, mix well, and store in a cool place.
2. Moisten the skin and scrub with the mixture, wash off.

Scrub for Sensitive Skin

Avocado is rich in natural oils that help moisturize skin. Cucumber is known for its oil removal properties and is also a natural coolant. It has skin whitening properties as well, and it gives relief to burns and other skin inflammations. Brown sugar is an excellent dead skin cell remover.

Makes: 12 ounces

Ingredients
1 medium cucumber, chopped
1 cup brown sugar
½ cup avocado oil

Directions
1. Blend the cucumber pieces in a blender until smooth.
2. In a bowl, combine the blended cucumber, avocado oil, and brown sugar.
3. Rub the mixture gently all over your body. Leave it on for 3-4 minutes.
4. Wash with lukewarm water.

Scrub for Soothing Sore Muscles

Epsom salt is known to soothe sore muscles because it contains magnesium. This invigorating combination of Epsom salt with shea butter and essential oils is sure to help remove stiffness and tension from your hard-working body.

Makes: 12 ounces

Ingredients
⅓ cup raw shea butter
¼ cup olive oil
½ teaspoon tangerine essential oil
20 drops lavender essential oil
20 drops eucalyptus essential oil
1 cup Epsom salts

Directions
1. Place the shea butter in a heatproof bowl and melt it in the microwave at 50% power.
2. Add the olive oil and mix.
3. Add the essential oils one at a time, mixing after each addition.
4. Pour in the Epsom salts and mix thoroughly.
5. To use, massage the scrub over sore muscles and rinse off. A scoop may be added to bathwater for a soothing soak.

Apple Spice Scrub

Gently exfoliate while leaving your skin smooth and soft, with the comforting scent of apple and cinnamon.

Makes: 20 ounces

Ingredients
1 cup of sugar
1 cup brown sugar
1 teaspoon apple pie spice
1 teaspoon cinnamon
½ - ¾ cup of coconut oil
6-10 drops apple essential oil (optional)

Directions
1. Combine all the ingredients together and mix well.
2. Massage on the skin and rinse off.

Anti-Cellulite Scrub

Take your basic coffee scrub to a higher level by adding sugar for better stimulation. This improves circulation, and with coffee's anti-cellulite and tightening effects, you'll have softer, smoother, younger-looking skin. The vanilla has anti-inflammatory properties, while its aroma helps you to relax.

Makes: 8 ounces

Ingredients
¼ cup finely ground dry coffee
½ cup sugar
½ teaspoon natural vanilla extract
2 tablespoons coconut oil
2 tablespoons castor oil

Directions
1. Mix the coffee, sugar, and vanilla in a bowl.
2. Gradually add the oils while mixing.
3. Apply to problem areas and rub in a circular motion. Rinse with warm water.

Body Lotions

All market lotions are not created equal! Creating your own at home is absolutely the best option.

Lotions are designed to moisturize the skin, but some store-bought brands can actually leave the skin drier than it was before. This can happen when the lotion is made up of inexpensive materials that do not, in fact, lock the moisture in. These lotions dissipate quickly, leaving your skin drier than before.

Body lotions are made up of three components. The first, the humectant component, sucks water from the air and into your skin. The second, the occlusive component, helps to seal in that moisture. The third component is designed to help your skin replenish itself.

Body lotions provide moisture for the skin and help to prevent cracking and chapping. Lotions are in the same family as creams, however, they're not quite as viscous. This low-viscosity factor means you can use them all over the body for total moisturizing. Lotions can also be easily applied after hand washing and will help your hands stay smooth and soft, and appear youthful.

Benefits

Body lotions are a great option for full-body moisturizing.

The lotions you will be making at home contain essential ingredients that hone in on what your skin needs and then replenish what's missing. Since you will be using only the best of ingredients, these high-quality lotions also seal your skin so you aren't losing any moisture, either.

The combination of the moisturizer with essential oils that are mood stabilizers and contain other properties to promote skin health make for a fantastic skincare product you can count on.

Storage

If possible, try to get yourself a pump bottle so you can avoid contamination. However, if you can't find one, you can use jars with airtight lids.

How to Do It Yourself

Creating body lotion at home is a snap. You only need a few simple ingredients and a blender, and soon you'll have gorgeous body lotion at a fraction of the cost of over-the-counter brands.

You will use a combination of the following ingredients:

Distilled water
Aloe Vera
Oil
Beeswax
Essential oil

What to Watch out For

Since we are trying to make these body lotions as clean and good for you as possible, we haven't included any of the chemicals that commercial brands use. However, that also means the lotions are more vulnerable to contamination. In order to prevent contamination, it is best to use a pump bottle. You should be able to find them easily on the web, or check your nearest discount or dollar store. If you do end up using a jar, make sure your hands are clean each time you use the product in order to minimize the chance of contamination. Also, make sure you dry your hands after washing them in order to avoid contaminating the lotion with water bacteria.

Body Lotion Recipes

Super Simple Luxurious Lotion

This particular lotion is a little heavier than your standard one, so you will need to place the lotion in a container as opposed to a pump bottle. The grapeseed oil extract is a natural preservative, meaning you can store this lotion for a lot longer than you would most homemade products.

Makes: 16 ounces

Ingredients
1 cup almond oil
½ cup coconut oil
½ cup beeswax
1 teaspoon vanilla extract
½ teaspoon grapeseed oil extract

Directions
1. Sterilize your containers.
2. Place the ingredients in a clean glass jar.
3. Create a water bath in a saucepan, and place the jar in the saucepan long enough to allow the ingredients to melt.
4. Mix the ingredients together, and pour the lotion in the sterilized containers. Allow it to set.
5. You can store this lotion, unopened, for up to approximately 6 months.

Lavender Lotion

There's something very soothing about the scent of lavender. Lavender in essential oil form is believed to help in mild cases of depression. Additionally, topical application of it promotes healing and is antiseptic.

Makes: 16 ounces

Ingredients
1 cup coconut oil
1 cup shea butter
2 teaspoons lavender essential oil

Directions
1. Sterilize your containers.
2. Place the ingredients in a clean glass jar.
3. Create a water bath in a saucepan, and place the jar in the saucepan long enough for the ingredients to melt.
4. Mix the ingredients together, and pour the lotion into your sterilized containers.

Aloe Lotion

Aloe is wonderfully soothing for irritated skin, and it is found in numerous commercial applications. The great news is that you can enjoy the healing benefits of aloe without the additional gunk that commercial products have, by mixing up your very own batch.

Makes: 14 ounces
Preparation time: 5 minutes

Ingredients
¼ cup pure aloe vera gel
1 cup coconut oil
½ cup grated beeswax
1 teaspoon vitamin E oil

Directions
1. Place the ingredients in a saucepan and heat over low heat.
2. As the ingredients melt, mix them together.
3. Once the ingredients are melted and combined, remove the pot to the counter, and let it rest for 10 minutes.
4. Place lotion for immediate use in a clean dispenser, and the remainder in a jar with an airtight lid.

Double Chocolate Lotion

The scent of this lotion is absolutely divine. Get yourself a tiny bottle and fill it up with lotion so you can carry it with you and apply it after washing your hands. This simple thing can help slow down the aging look of hands.

Makes: 14 ounces
Preparation time: 5 minutes

Ingredients
1 teaspoon cocoa essential oil
½ cup pure distilled water
½ cup cocoa butter
½ cup jojoba oil
½ cup grated beeswax
1 teaspoon vitamin E oil

Directions
1. Place the ingredients in saucepan and heat over low heat.
2. As the ingredients melt, mix them together.
3. Once the ingredients are melted and combined, remove the pot to the counter and let it rest for 10 minutes.
4. Place lotion for immediate use in a dispenser, and the remainder in a jar with an airtight lid.

Raspberry Almond Lotion

Raspberry seed oil is a powerhouse of antioxidants and includes the wonderfully beneficial Omega-3 and Omega-6 oils. Make sure you are buying raspberry seed oil, and not raspberry oil, as there is no such natural product in existence, so you will be slathering your body with synthetic raspberry.

Makes: 14 ounces
Preparation time: 5 minutes

Ingredients
2 teaspoons raspberry seed oil
¼ cup pure aloe vera gel
1 cup almond oil
½ cup grated beeswax
1 teaspoon vitamin E oil

Directions
1. Place all the ingredients in a saucepan and heat over low heat.
2. As the ingredients melt, stir continuously until well mixed.
3. Once the ingredients are melted and combined, remove the pot to the counter and let it rest for 10 minutes.
4. Place lotion for immediate use in a dispenser, and the remainder in a jar with an airtight lid.

Grapefruit Zing Lotion

Say "Good morning!" to yourself with the refreshing scent of grapefruit. This scent not only packs a punch, but the essential oil helps you avoid getting those aesthetically worrying pimples.

Makes: 14 ounces
Preparation time: 5 minutes

Ingredients
1 teaspoon grapefruit essential oil
¼ cup pure aloe vera gel
1 cup coconut oil
½ cup grated beeswax
1 teaspoon vitamin E oil

Directions
1. Place all the ingredients in a saucepan, and heat them over low heat.
2. As the ingredients melt, mix them together.
3. Once the ingredients are melted, remove the pot to the counter and let it rest for 10 minutes.
4. Place lotion for immediate use in a dispenser, and the remainder in a jar with an airtight lid.

Calamine Moisturizer

Calamine lotion is a multipurpose lotion, which can be used for sunburns, insect bites, and dressing wounds. Bentonite clay helps in healing wounds faster. Baking soda helps relieve itching and skin irritation, and tea tree oil soothes inflamed or itchy skin. Sea salt helps reduce swelling and removes dead skin cells, while pink kaolin clay is helpful for sensitive skin. It is also an excellent exfoliator, and it gives color to the lotion. Glycerine helps absorb moisture into the skin.

Makes: 12 ounces
Preparation time: 5 minutes

Ingredients:
⅓ cup baking soda
¼ cup sea salt
⅓ cup bentonite clay
10 teaspoons kaolin clay
1 cup water, or more if required
40 drops tea tree essential oil
4 teaspoons glycerine (optional)

Directions
1. Mix together the baking soda, salt, bentonite clay, and kaolin in a bowl.
2. Add water and stir constantly to form a paste. You may add more water if required, until the desired consistency is achieved.
3. Add the tea tree oil and glycerine and mix well.
4. Store in an airtight jar in a cool and dry place.

Baby Lotion

Coconut oil is a great natural moisturizer, which helps fight wrinkles and deeply nourishes your skin. Aloe vera has anti-inflammatory and moisturizing properties. Olive oil and vitamin E oil work wonders for soft, supple, and younger-looking skin. Lanolin helps cure skin abrasions and also deeply moisturizes your skin.

Makes: 16 ounces
Preparation time: 5 minutes

Ingredients
1 cup water
¼ cup olive oil
2 tablespoons coconut oil
2 tablespoons beeswax, grated
1 vitamin E capsule
1 tablespoon shea butter or cocoa butter
½ teaspoon aloe vera gel
½ teaspoon 100% lanolin

Directions
1. Sterilize your containers.
2. Place the ingredients in a clean glass jar.
3. Create a water bath in a saucepan, and place the jar in it long enough to allow the ingredients to melt.
4. Mix all the ingredients together, and place in your sterilized containers.

Sleep Time Lotion

This lotion is very helpful for people with insomnia. Chamomile is an anti-inflammatory and has antibacterial properties. It helps heal rough and damaged skin. It has properties that help you soothe your mind and relax your senses. The soothing smell of lavender helps you to relax and fall asleep faster, and it reduces stress. Jojoba oil helps to keep the skin softer.

Makes: 12 ounces
Preparation time: 3 hours

Ingredients
2 ½ teaspoons chamomile flowers
2 ½ teaspoons lavender buds
3 ounces liquid jojoba oil
4 ounces distilled water, heated
1 ½ ounces coconut oil
¾ ounce beeswax, grated
10 drops chamomile essential oil
10 drops lavender essential oil
Cheesecloth

Directions
1. To infuse the jojoba oil, place the chamomile flowers and lavender buds in a clean jar, such as a Mason jar. Pour the jojoba oil on top. Cover tightly with a well-fitting lid.
2. Create a water bath in a saucepan and place the jar in the simmering water. Let it sit in the simmering water bath for about 2 hours. Remove it from the heat and let it cool down. Strain the infused oil through a piece of cheesecloth. Discard the flowers and the buds.
3. Pour the strained jojoba oil into the top of a double-boiler, and mix in the coconut oil and beeswax. Stir frequently until they are melted and well combined.

4. Remove the pot from the heat and let the mixture cool to body temperature, stirring occasionally.
5. Pour the hot distilled water in a tall container. Place a stick blender in the container, running on low speed.
6. With the blender running slowly, pour the infused oil in a thin drizzle into the container. It will slowly become creamy.
7. Add the essential oils. Stop the blender when you reach the consistency you desire.
8. Spoon it into an airtight container, and store it in a cool and dry place.

Calendula Lotion

Calendula helps heal wounds and cuts faster. Beeswax actively fights acne and pimple-causing bacteria. It is a natural skin moisturizer that keeps your skin soft and supple. Glycerine is one of the best natural ingredients to moisturize your skin, and grapeseed oil is a natural preservative and has anti-wrinkle properties.

Makes: 18 ounces
Preparation time: 2 ½ hours

Ingredients
5-6 handfuls Calendula fresh flowers OR about 5-6 teaspoons dried
8 ounces jojoba oil
8 ounces distilled water
1 ounce witch hazel
1 ounce beeswax
1 ounce glycerine
½ teaspoon grapefruit seed extract (optional)
20 drops lavender essential oil (optional)
10 drops rosemary essential oil

Directions
1. To infuse the oil, place half the calendula flowers in a clean jar, like a Mason jar. Pour in the jojoba oil. Place the lid and tightly close it.
2. Create a water bath in a saucepan, and place the jar in the saucepan. Let it remain in the water bath, simmering, for about 2 hours.
3. Once it is infused, strain it through a piece of cheesecloth. Discard the flowers.
4. Meanwhile, prepare the infused water. Place the remaining calendula flowers in a bowl. Pour boiling

distilled water over them, and allow it to steep. When it cools to room temperature, strain out the flowers and discard them.

5. In a heat-resistant bowl, combine the witch hazel, infused jojoba oil, beeswax, and glycerine. Place the bowl over the water bath.
6. Allow the ingredients to melt, and mix thoroughly.
7. Remove the bowl from the water bath.
8. Add the infused water. With an immersion blender set on low, start mixing.
9. It will start getting creamy. Add the rosemary essential oil, and the lavender essential oil if you are using it, and the grapefruit seed extract. Stop the blender when you reach the consistency you desire.
10. Transfer into an airtight jar.

Ultra-Moisturizing Lotion

Shea butter is well known for its skin moisturizing properties. It helps reduce wrinkles and also treats eczema and other such skin conditions. Tea tree oil is an antibacterial that helps fight pimples and maintain blemish-free skin. The essential oils help soothe the skin and also relax the senses. Almond oil is rich in vitamin E, which can very well be called an elixir for younger-looking skin.

Makes: 12 ounces
Preparation time: 30 minutes

Ingredients
1 cup shea butter
¼ cup avocado oil OR sweet almond oil OR jojoba oil
30 drops lavender essential oil
20 drops rosemary essential oil
15 drops carrot seed oil
10 drops tea tree oil

Directions
1. Place a saucepan over medium-low heat. Add the shea butter and the oil of your choice. When they have melted, stir to combine, and then remove the mixture from the heat, and transfer it into a bowl.
2. Place the bowl in the freezer to cool for about 15-20 minutes until it is slightly solid.
3. Add the lavender oil, rosemary oil, carrot seed oil, and tea tree oil. Whisk until the mixture is creamy. (You can use the whisk attachment of your mixer or you can use a hand whisk.)
4. Spoon the lotion into a clean, dry jar. Store it in a cool and dry place at room temperature.
5. Apply on the body, or the face, whenever required.

Organic Homemade Lotion Bar

Lotion bars are like soap. They're solid at room temperature, but when you hold and massage it the way you would soap, the heat from your hands melts enough of the bar to coat your skin. These make very fancy gifts.

Coconut oil is known for its skin nourishing and wrinkle fighting abilities. Shea butter is a natural moisturizer that is one of the best natural skin care ingredients. Vitamin E helps rebuild skin cells and keeps your skin soft, supple, and looking younger. Beeswax helps fights acne and also skin conditions like eczema and psoriasis.

Makes: 24 ounces
Preparation time: 5 minutes

Ingredients
8 ounces coconut oil
8 ounces shea butter OR cocoa butter OR mango butter, OR a mixture of the 3 butters
8 ounces beeswax, or more if you like a thicker consistency
3 teaspoons vitamin E oil
10-15 drops essential oil of your choice

Directions
1. Mix all the ingredients together, except the essential oil and vitamin E oil, in a heat-resistant glass bowl.
2. Boil some water in a saucepan and place the bowl on top when the water is simmering. Allow the ingredients to melt.
3. Add the essential oil and vitamin E oil.
4. Mix the ingredients gently with your hands, and pour it into molds of the desired size and shape.
5. Let it cool completely before removing it out of the mold.

Nourishing Hand and Body Lotion

Shea butter and coconut oil are excellent natural skin moisturizers that help you maintain soft and supple skin. Coconut oil deeply nourishes skin. Aloe vera helps fight skin inflammation and has antibacterial properties.

Makes: 12 ounces
Preparation time: 5 minutes

Ingredients
½ cup coconut oil
¼ cup shea butter
¼ cup cocoa butter
2 tablespoons aloe vera juice
2 tablespoons jojoba oil
10 drops essential oil of your choice

Directions
1. Combine the coconut oil, shea butter, and cocoa butter in a saucepan. Place the saucepan over low heat. When the ingredients have melted, remove it from the heat.
2. Add the aloe vera, jojoba oil, and essential oil. Whisk well until you get the desired consistency.
3. Transfer the mixture into an airtight container, and store it in a cool, dry place.

Nourishing Rose and Almond Moisturizer

Shea butter, cocoa butter and coconut oil are excellent natural skin moisturizers that help you maintain soft and supple skin. Almond oil helps nourish the skin from within and it reduces fine lines and wrinkles.

Makes: 12 ounces
Preparation time: 5 minutes

Ingredients
½ cup coconut oil
¼ cup shea butter
¼ cup cocoa butter
2 tablespoons rose water
2 tablespoons almond oil
10 drops rose essential oil

Directions
1. Combine the coconut oil, shea butter, and cocoa butter in a saucepan. Place the pan over low heat. When the ingredients are melted, remove it from the heat.
2. Add the rose water, almond oil, and rose essential oil. Whisk well until you get the desired consistency.
3. Transfer the mixture into an airtight container, and store it in a cool, dry place.

Face Creams

Most often, the quality of one's skin is gauged by that of our face. When we speak of one's complexion, we refer to the skin on the face. We are willing to spend money on products that will keep our faces looking young, clean, soft, and beautiful. God forbid we put any strong, cancer-causing chemicals on the precious skin of the face! The sad truth, though, is that we do. Such dangerous ingredients as phthalates, parabens, perfumes, preservatives, and dyes are staples even in the most expensive creams. The skin on our face is thinner and more delicate than the rest of the body, and it should not be subjected to harsh ingredients. By making your own face creams, you can be sure that the ingredients are pure and safe. You can adjust ingredients and proportions to suit your needs perfectly and to make sure that only the best goes on your face.

Benefits

Those who have tried making their own face creams are surprised at how simple, inexpensive and effective they are!

You will have a hand at choosing the best ingredients, sans harmful chemicals, to suit your needs, and you'll be rewarded with a softer, younger-looking, smooth, and healthy complexion.

Many say it seems challenging at first, but the results are well worth it in the end. The best part is that you can come up with a concoction that works best for you!

What You Need

Here's an introductory list of ingredients you can use to know exactly what to choose for your skin type. Combining these, you can keep the skin on your face the way you want it.

Anti-Acne
Aloe Vera gel
Tea Tree Oil

Anti-Aging Essential Oils
Almond Oil
Clary Sage
Green Tea
Helichrysum
Myrrh
Rosehip Seed Oil

Anti-Inflammatory
Aloe Vera Gel
Green Tea
Witch Hazel Water

Anti-Puffiness
Almond Oil

Anti-Wrinkles
Grapeseed Oil
Vitamin E Oil
Apricot Seed Oil

Astringent
Lemon Essential Oil
Witch Hazel Water

Lighteners
Aloe Vera Gel
Honey
Kojic acid
Lemon Essential Oil
Licorice extract
Turmeric

Detoxifiers
Bentonite Clay
Lemon Essential Oil

Moisturizers
Grapeseed Oil
Jojoba Oil
Shea Butter
Rosehip Seed Oil
Extra Virgin Coconut Oil

Natural Tint
Mineral Clay
Cocoa Powder

Pore-Tightener
Grape Seed Oil

Skin Healing and Repair
Aloe Vera Gel
Extra-Virgin Coconut Oil
Rosehip Seed Oil
Vitamin E Oil

Stabilizer
Beeswax
Aloe Vera Gel

Sun Protection
Green Tea
Vitamin E Oil

Storage

Use airtight, non-reactive containers like glass jars. The storage life of a product depends on the usage, and sources of contamination. These should usually last, refrigerated, in sterilized airtight glass jars for at least a month. Throw them out if you notice any odd odor.

How to Do It Yourself

You'll need these things to make your face creams:
Chocolate melter or double-boiler
Blender or hand mixer
Mason jars
Heatproof and non-reactive bowls, measuring cups and ladles, spoons or spatulas
Pipettes

What to Watch out For

When mixing water-based ingredients (like aloe gel) with waxes and oils, make sure they are of the same temperature and a little higher than room temperature, to avoid separation.

Lemon essential oil and other citrus essential oils can cause sun sensitivity, so these are best left out of the concoction if you intend to use it during daytime.

Take particular note of the comedogenic ratings of oil ingredients – how likely a substance is to block the pores. On a scale 0 to 5, 0 would mean that it is unlikely to clog the pores (non-comedogenic) while 5 would be the most likely to clog and therefore worsen any acne condition or skin irritation. Oils can be used in combinations to avail of the benefits, while avoiding the clogging of pores. Here are the comedogenic ratings of some common oils and waxes for facial creams.

0	Argan Oil
	Shea Butter
1	Calendula Oil
	Castor Oil
	Rosehip Oil
2	Almond Oil
	Sunflower Oil
	Beeswax
	Emulsifying Wax
	Grapeseed Oil
	Jojoba Oil
	Olive Oil
	Evening Primrose Oil
4	Cocoa Butter
	Coconut Oil

As always, check for any possible allergic reactions or sensitivity to ingredients before use.

Face Cream Recipes

Rejuvenating Night Cream

The healing, moisturizing, anti-aging and lightening effects of this cream will reveal a youthful complexion. To make it into a day cream, simply eliminate the lemon essential oil. This concoction contains bentonite clay, a healing clay known to remove toxins. With bentonite clay as an ingredient, make sure that the cream does not come in contact with any metal, as it causes metals to leach out.

Makes: 3.5 ounces
Preparation time: 45 minutes

Ingredients
¼ cup aloe vera gel
1 teaspoon vitamin E oil
1 teaspoon honey
5-10 drops lemon essential oil
½ teaspoon beeswax granules
1 teaspoon coconut oil
2 tablespoons almond oil
½ teaspoon shea butter
½ teaspoon bentonite clay

Directions
1. Combine the aloe vera gel, vitamin E oil, honey, and lemon essential oil in a bowl, mixing well. Set it aside.
2. Melt the beeswax, coconut oil, almond oil, and shea butter. This may be done at low power in a microwave, over a double boiler, or in a slow cooker.

3. If you are using a hand mixer, leave this mixture in the bowl and let it cool. Otherwise, transfer it into a blender and allow it to solidify.
4. Break up the solidified oil and wax mixture with a spoon, and add the aloe vera mixture. Blend well.
5. Transfer the cream to a glass or plastic bowl, and stir in the bentonite clay.
6. Store it in a glass or plastic container in a cool, dry place.

Anti-Acne Cream with Grapeseed Oil

Grapeseed oil is known to tighten pores and reduce oiliness while protecting the skin's natural oil barrier. Cedarwood essential oil lends its anti-inflammatory and antiseptic properties. The other ingredients, like witch hazel, vitamin E, aloe vera, and grapefruit seed extract all add to the acne-fighting and skin-conditioning qualities of this cream. Stearic acid can be of animal or plant origin, and adds to texture without adding to greasiness.

Makes: 4 ounces
Preparation time: 10 minutes plus cooling time

Ingredients
4 teaspoons grapeseed oil
1 tablespoon emulsifying wax
½ teaspoon stearic acid
½ teaspoon vitamin E oil
⅓ cup witch hazel (liquid)
1 tablespoon aloe vera gel
5 drops grapefruit seed extract
5 drops lemon or lavender essential oil
1 drop cedarwood essential oil

Directions
1. Sterilize dark, glass jars.
2. Combine the grapeseed oil, emulsifying wax, and stearic acid in a heatproof bowl or double boiler.
3. Heat gently over boiling water until the wax has melted.
4. Remove the mixture from the heat and add the vitamin E oil. Stir, and set it aside.
5. To prevent separation in the mixture, the witch hazel must not be cold when added to the oil mixture. To warm it, combine it with the aloe vera gel in a heatproof container, place it over the double boiler, and heat to lukewarm.

6. Whisk the warmed witch hazel mixture while gradually pouring in the oil mixture in a thin stream.
7. Continue whisking while adding the grape seed extract and the essential oils.
8. Pour the mixture into the sterilized, dark jars and let it cool. Stir occasionally to prevent separation.
9. Place the lids on when the mixture is completely cooled, and store it away from heat and light.
10. Apply on the face as a night cream after cleansing.

Anti-Aging Face Cream with Rose Water, Wheat Germ & Honey

Shea butter restores the skin's moisture, while rose water rejuvenates the skin. Honey and beeswax will retain the moisture, and also help fight signs of aging. Wheat germ tightens skin cells and improves elasticity.

Makes: 7-8 ounces
Preparation time:

Ingredients
8 teaspoons beeswax, grated
4 tablespoons rose water
4 teaspoons organic honey
¼ cup shea butter
8 teaspoons wheat germ oil
4 tablespoons sweet almond oil
10 drops carrot seed oil
10 drops rose oil, or any essential oil of your choice

Directions
1. Sterilize your containers.
2. Place the beeswax in a glass container. Place the container in a double boiler on low heat.
3. Pour the rose water into a separate cup, and place the cup in the double boiler, along with the beeswax. Similarly, warm the honey it its own container.
4. When the beeswax is melted, add the shea butter and stir constantly until it melts and is well blended. Add the wheat germ oil and sweet almond oil. Whip it with a whisk or an immersion blender until everything is thoroughly combined.

5. Keep mixing, while you add the warm rose water and warm honey, and continue to stir while the mixture cools down.
6. Add the carrot seed oil and rose oil, and stir to combine.
7. Transfer the mixture to your clean containers, and label them.

Anti-Wrinkle Face Cream

The rosehip seed oil in this concoction will work its regenerative and moisturizing powers on your face! Rosehip seed oil is said to enhance elastin and collagen production in the skin, helping erase fine lines and wrinkles.

Makes: 1.5 ounces
Preparation time: 45 minutes

Ingredients
2 teaspoons jojoba oil
1 teaspoon coconut oil
3 teaspoons apricot kernel oil
3 teaspoons rosehip seed oil
1 ½ teaspoons beeswax pastilles
6-10 teaspoons rose-water

Directions
1. Place all the ingredients EXCEPT the rose water in a double boiler.
2. Heat until melted (about 5 minutes).
3. Remove the bowl from the heat and let it cool until it is comfortable to handle, but not solidified.
4. Carefully transfer the mixture to a blender, and pulse while adding the rose water gradually.
5. You should get a light, creamy mixture. Store it in a clean airtight container, in a cool place.

Moisturizer and Makeup Remover

Here's a moisturizer that's simple to make and chemical-free. It protects skin from dryness and also acts as a makeup remover.

Makes: 18 ounces

Ingredients
¾ ounce (by weight) beeswax pastilles, unscented, cosmetic grade
¼ cup sunflower oil
¼ cup coconut oil
1 cup aloe vera gel
10 drops chamomile OR lavender essential oil

Directions
1. Melt the beeswax, sunflower oil, and coconut oil in a double boiler or chocolate melter.
2. Pour the heated mixture into a blender, and let it cool to just a bit warmer than room temperature. It should look like a thick oil.
3. If the aloe vera is cold, gently warm it to lukewarm. You may do this over a double boiler or by placing it in a heatproof glass measuring cup over hot water.
4. Stir the essential oil into the heated aloe vera gel.
5. The wax and aloe vera mixture should both be lukewarm at this point. Adding cold aloe vera to the wax mixture will result in separation.
6. Start blending the wax mixture, scraping the bottom to ensure thorough blending.
7. Very gradually, pour in the aloe vera mixture while blending. The mixture will turn into a white, fluffy cream.
8. Keep a small amount for use and store the rest in the refrigerator.

Anti-Puffiness Face Cream

This cream will remove the puffiness and dark circles under your eyes. The caffeine in green tea constricts blood vessels to reduce swelling, and it also soothes inflammation and irritation. Almond oil reduces puffiness and discoloration. It will also nourish your skin and help soften or erase wrinkles. Then there's the cell-regenerative property of rosehip seed oil, and the potent moisturizing and soothing effect of carrot seed oil. It's chock-full of benefits!

Makes: 4 ounces

Ingredients
1 teaspoon emulsifying wax
1 tablespoon rosehip seed oil
¼ teaspoon vitamin E oil
1 tablespoon sweet almond oil
¼ cup brewed green tea
1 drop carrot seed essential oil
3 drops choice of essential oil (chamomile, lavender or rose)

Directions
1. Sterilize all equipment that will come in contact with the ingredients by wiping it down with rubbing alcohol and leaving it to dry completely before use.
2. Prepare two glass bowls and two medium-sized pans.
3. Fill the pans halfway with water and place them over the stovetop.
4. To one bowl, add the wax, rosehip seed oil, vitamin E oil, and sweet almond oil.
5. Pour the brewed green tea into the other bowl.
6. Place one bowl over each water-filled pan and turn on to medium heat.

7. Heat to 130°F. The content of both bowls should be the same temperature, or else the cream will not set.
8. Pour the green tea into the wax mixture.
9. Whip the mixture with a handheld mixer or blender.
10. Blending should be intermittent and can take 30 minutes to an hour before the water is no longer separated from the oils.
11. When it reaches a light, creamy consistency, stir in the carrot seed and other essential oils.
12. Pour into sterilized containers.

NOTE: The relatively high water content of this cream may cause it to spoil easily. Discard it if there are any molds or if a cheesy odor can be detected. An organic preservative of choice may be added, if desired. Follow the packaging instructions for quantity and directions.

Apricot Moisture Cream for Sensitive Skin

Apricot seed oil is great for sensitive skin because it's non-irritating, but gently moisturizing and nourishing. The ingredients are either non-comedogenic or have a low comedogenic rating, and are therefore perfect for sensitive skin!

Makes: 3 ounces

Ingredients
3 tablespoons shea butter
3 tablespoons apricot seed oil
½ teaspoon vitamin E oil
1 teaspoon aloe vera gel
5 drops chamomile OR rose OR neroli essential oils

Directions
1. Using a blender or mixer with a wire whip attachment, whip the shea butter to a fluffy consistency.
2. Gradually add the other ingredients while whipping.
3. Transfer the mixture to a clean jar, cover tightly, and label.

Body Butters

Body butter is intended to be as decadent as it sounds. It provides your skin with a full blast of moisture, thanks to the high oil content. Body butters differ from lotions in that they are much thicker and are able to provide your skin with a thicker barrier against moisture loss.

Body butters have been known since Roman times. Those body butters are similar in composition to the recipes provided in this book in that the ingredients are all natural without the harmful preservatives found in commercial products.

We've used a variety of butters including shea butter, mango butter, and coconut butter as the base for our body butter recipes. These butters contain essential vitamins and antioxidants that are not only replenishing, but also healing. The high viscosity levels make the butters quite dense and perfect for very dry areas. It is also a good idea to give your whole body the body butter treatment once a week to get amazingly soft, supple skin all over.

Benefits

Body butters provide ultimate moisturizing for ultimate beauty. They are composed of humectants and occlusive agents like body lotions but the composition in butters comes in at a ratio that really takes their effect on the skin right off the charts.

Common humectants found in body butter include honey and glycerine. These do the heavy lifting when it comes to luring moisture from the air into your skin.

Common occlusives include shea butter and silicone. The occlusives are your official skin guards, which ensure that once the moisture has made its way into your skin, it stays there.

Storage

Use mason jars or another type of jar with an airtight lid to store your body butters. You should sterilize the jars in a water bath prior to filling and sealing them. Once sealed, store them in a cool place.

How to Do It Yourself

Body butters are simple to make at home and require little time. Standard body butters include a combination of the following elements:
Butter
Oil
Essential oil

What to Watch out For

The thick consistency of body butter means you need to use jars for storage, and of course, that means contamination is possible. It is best to store your butter in smaller jars so the chance of contamination per jar is less. Also ensure that you have clean, dry hands before you stick your hand into one of the jars to scoop out some body butter, or use a clean spoon.

Body Butter Recipes

Hawaiian Body Butter

Slather summer on your body with this body butter scented with pineapple and mango. The mango butter is wonderfully rich. Its anti-aging properties can reduce those irritating lines that begin to appear as you age. The mango butter combined with coconut oil and Vitamin E will have you feeling lovely and soft.

Makes: 12 ounces

Ingredients
1 teaspoon pineapple essential oil
½ cup mango butter
1 cup coconut oil
1 teaspoon vitamin E oil

Directions
1. Place the ingredients in a glass bowl and beat until smooth.
2. Scoop the butter into sterilized jars and store it in a cool place.

Mandarin Chocolate Body Butter

Raise your hands if you absolutely love the heavenly scent of mandarin spiked with chocolate! This body butter is fantastic on the skin. The natural scents provide a mood boost that will have you whipping through the morning and afternoon in a sweet haze.

Makes: 12 ounces

Ingredients
1 teaspoon mandarin zest
1 teaspoon cocoa essential oil
1 ½ cups coconut butter*

Directions
1. Place the ingredients in a glass bowl and beat them until smooth.
2. Scoop the butter into sterilized jars, and store it in a cool place.

*Note: You can make your own coconut butter by processing unsweetened, shredded coconut in a food processor until it is completely smooth.

Strawberry Vanilla Butter

Stay sweet all day long with lovely strawberry-and-vanilla-infused butter. Strawberries contain ellagic acid, which helps spur the production of collagen and in turn ensures you age more slowly. As in the case of raspberry seed essential oil, there is no such thing as strawberry essential oil, so you must be sure to purchase only strawberry seed essential oil to ensure you're getting an all-natural product.

Makes: 16 ounces

Ingredients
2 teaspoons strawberry seed essential oil
1 cup shea butter
½ cup coconut oil
½ cup jojoba oil

Directions
1. Fill a saucepan halfway up with water and heat over medium.
2. Grab a glass bowl that will fit over the mouth of the saucepan.
3. Place the shea butter and coconut oil in the glass bowl, and stir until they are melted.
4. Remove the bowl and place it on a cool surface. Add the oils, stir, and cool the mixture in the refrigerator for half an hour.
5. Once the mixture is cool, use a hand immersion blender to beat the butter until it is creamy.
6. Scoop the butter into clean jars with airtight lids, and store it in a cool place until use.

Golden Body Butter

Oh how she glows and she glows. You will glow after using this butter, thanks to the cocoa powder and honey combination, which creates a slightly sun-kissed look.

Makes: 16 ounces

Ingredients
2 tablespoons cocoa powder
2 tablespoons raw honey
1 cup shea butter
½ cup coconut oil
½ cup jojoba oil

Directions
1. Fill a saucepan halfway up with water and heat it over medium.
2. Grab a glass bowl that will fit over the mouth of the saucepan.
3. Place the shea butter and coconut oil in the glass bowl, and stir until melted.
4. Remove the bowl and place it on a cool surface.
5. Add the remaining ingredients, stir, and cool the mixture in the refrigerator for half an hour. Once it is cool, use a hand immersion blender to beat the butter until it is creamy.
6. Scoop the butter into clean jars with airtight lids and store them in a cool place until use.

Mango Body Butter

This simple, rich butter is great to use in the winter. After taking a shower, slather it all over your feet, don your socks, and wake up in the morning with feet so soft you'll feel as though you can float!

Makes: 14 ounces

Ingredients
1 cup mango butter
½ cup coconut oil
1 teaspoon vitamin E oil
2 tablespoons aloe gel

Directions
1. Fill a saucepan halfway up with water and heat it over medium.
2. Grab a glass bowl that will fit over the mouth of the saucepan.
3. Place the mango butter and coconut oil in the glass bowl, and stir until it melts.
4. Remove the bowl and place it on a cool surface.
5. Add the remaining ingredients, stir, and cool the mixture in the refrigerator for half an hour. Once the mixture is cool, use a hand immersion blender to beat the butter until it is creamy.
6. Scoop the butter into clean jars with airtight lids and store it in a cool place until use.

Cinnamon Body Butter

The comfy scent of cinnamon can make you feel at home wherever you are. When used in a lotion, it will give you that same feeling of cozy comfort. With its anti-bacterial properties, cinnamon is also wonderful for the skin. It's soothing for the joints as well as the skin.

Makes: 12 ounces

Ingredients
1 cup cocoa butter
½ cup argan oil
1 teaspoon cinnamon essential oil
1 teaspoon Arabica seed oil

Directions
1. Fill a saucepan halfway up with water and heat it over medium.
2. Grab a glass bowl that will fit over the mouth of the saucepan.
3. Place the cocoa butter and coconut oil in the glass bowl, and stir until they are melted.
4. Remove the bowl and place it on a cool surface.
5. Add the remaining ingredients, stir, and cool in refrigerator for half an hour.
6. Once the mixture is cool, use a hand immersion blender to beat the butter until it is creamy.
7. Scoop the butter into jars with airtight lids and store in a cool place until use.

Citrus Body Butter for Glowing skin

Tea tree oil is an anti-bacterial, and the extra virgin coconut oil and shea butter will provide your skin with the moisture it needs throughout the day. The orange essential oil will keep your mind fresh and alert.

Makes: 35 ounces.

Ingredients
3 cups extra virgin coconut oil
10 ½ ounces shea butter
5 drops tea tree oil
20 drops sweet orange essential oil
20 drops lemon essential oil

Directions
1. Mix the shea butter and coconut oil in a jar, such as a Mason jar. Cover the jar tightly with a lid.
2. Create a water bath in a saucepan and place the jar in the water. Allow all the ingredients to melt.
3. Remove the pot from the heat and add the tea tree oil and essential oils. Mix well and cool for about 30 minutes.
4. Freeze the mixture for 10-15 minutes or more. When the oils start solidifying, remove it from the freezer and whip it with a whisk until you get a light buttery consistency.
5. Spoon the butter into a clean jar. Close the lid tightly and place it in a cool, dry area.

Vanilla Bean Body Butter

This body butter will make you feel rejuvenated throughout the day, thanks to the pleasant and soothing aroma of vanilla. It also helps relax the body and mind. The cocoa butter helps to deeply nourish the skin, and the almond oil provides it with much-needed vitamin E.

Makes: 16 ounces

Ingredients
1 cup raw cocoa butter
½ cup sweet almond oil
½ cup coconut oil
2 vanilla bean pods

Directions
1. Combine the cocoa butter and coconut oil in a pan. Place the pan over low heat. When the ingredients are melted, remove it from the heat and set it aside to cool.
2. Grind the vanilla beans in a coffee grinder or food processor.
3. Add the sweet almond oil and ground vanilla beans to the cooled cocoa butter and coconut oil mixture. Mix well and freeze for about 20-25 minutes.
4. Whip the mixture in a food processor until buttery and creamy.
5. Scoop the butter into a glass jar with a lid. Refrigerate and use when necessary.

Aloe Vera Body Butter

Aloe vera soothes the skin and prevents skin inflammation. The three butters in this recipe will provide your skin with much-needed moisture and will keep it soft and supple. The essential oils will relax your mind and body. The grapeseed oil and beeswax will help prevent skin conditions like rashes, eczema, and acne.

Makes: 30 ounces

Ingredients
6 ounces shea butter
4 ounces mango butter
2 ounces coconut butter
2 ounces coconut oil
6 ounces grapeseed oil
1 ounce beeswax
4 ounces distilled water
4 ounces aloe Vera gel
40 drops sweet orange essential oil
40 drops patchouli essential oil
20 drops lavender essential oil

Directions
1. Sterilize your jars.
2. Mix the shea butter, mango butter, coconut butter, coconut oil, grapeseed oil, and beeswax in a heatproof glass bowl.
3. Create a water bath in a saucepan and place the bowl over the saucepan. Allow all the ingredients to melt.
4. Remove the mixture from the heat and let it cool for a while.
5. Place an immersion blender or hand mixer in the bowl. Let it run on low speed.

6. Slowly pour in the water and aloe vera gel. The mixture will become homogenous and creamy once you start blending. Continue blending until it mixes well.
7. Add the essential oils. Mix well until you reach the desired consistency.
8. Spoon the butter into the sterilized jars. Close the lids tightly and store in a cool and dry place.

Stretch Mark Lightening Body Butter

Regular use of this butter helps to lighten stretch marks.

Makes: 22 ounces

Ingredients
1 cup cocoa butter
1 cup shea butter
6 tablespoons almond oil
6 tablespoons olive oil
20 drops of lavender essential oil
20 drops of geranium essential oil
20 drops of patchouli essential oil

Directions
1. Combine the shea butter and cocoa butter in a heatproof glass bowl.
2. Prepare a water bath in a saucepan. Place the bowl over the saucepan when the water is simmering. Let the butters melt. When they are completely melted, slowly add the almond oil and olive oil. Stir well. Remove the mixture from the heat and cool for about half an hour.
3. Add the essential oils. Stir well.
4. Place the mixture in the freezer for a while.
5. When the oils begin to solidify slightly, whip them with a whisk or an immersion blender until you get a buttery consistency.
6. Scoop it into a glass jar. Cover tightly with a lid.
7. Store in a cool and dry place.

Rosemary Mint Whipped Shea Body Butter

This body butter provides long lasting moisture, and is ideal for dry and chapped skin. The kukui nut oil, extracted from the Hawaiian native tree Aleurites moluccans, also known as the candlenut tree, helps soothe and soften the skin, and provides relief from eczema and psoriasis as well as sunburns. The spearmint and rosemary oil will sharpen your senses and keep you feeling fresh all day long.
Makes: 30 ounces

Ingredients
6 ounces cocoa butter
18 ounces shea butter
6 ounces kukui nut oil
50 drops spearmint essential oil
40 drops rosemary essential oil

Directions
1. In a heatproof glass bowl, mix the cocoa butter, shea butter and kukui nut oil.
2. Place the bowl in a water bath over low heat.
3. When the butters are melted, remove the bowl from the heat. Set it aside to cool at room temperature.
4. Place it in the freezer for about 20 minutes, until it is almost solidified.
5. Whisk the mixture with a metal whisk or an immersion blender on low speed, and freeze it again for 15-20 minutes. The color will start getting creamy.
6. Whisk again and place it in the freezer if necessary until the mixture is chilled and has reached the desired consistency.
7. Add the essential oils. Mix well.
8. Spoon it into glass jars, and store it in a cool and dark place.

Lip Care

The lips need special care, as the skin in this area is especially thin and delicate. Unknowingly, we actually put dangerous substances on our lips that dry them out, darken them, damage them or cause them to absorb harmful toxins. Our lips are continuously subjected to beatings from chemicals in lipsticks, balms, cigarettes, and pollutants. Even sunlight, cold weather, and air conditioning can be damaging.

Many ingredients in commercial lip care products harm the lips more than they supposedly help them. Camphor, menthol, petroleum, parabens, salicylic acid, and perfumes are some examples. The lip products that we buy may seem helpful, but many of them dry out the skin on our lips even more.

The least we can do for our lips is to reduce the amount of toxins we expose them to by using only natural, chemical-free lip care products. By keeping the skin on our lips soft, moist and naturally pinkish, we not only improve our looks but contribute to our overall health and wellbeing.

Benefits

The ingredients used to make homemade lip care products keep the lips hydrated without suffocating them. They nourish and protect the lips and help restore them to their original youthful condition. Even if they may not go back to resembling baby lips, they'll be pampered and protected from the toxins often found in commercial products. These toxins can cause a number of health problems ranging from dryness, irritation, allergies, liver damage, hormonal imbalance, neurological damage, and even cancer. Natural oils are kind to the lips, acting as moisturizers, antioxidants, sun protection and anti-inflammatories. These oils encourage the skin on the lips to produce its own natural oils that form a protective barrier.

Using your own homemade lip care products is just one step to reducing exposure to harmful substances. What's more, by making your own concoctions, you can adjust the colors, flavors, and textures to come up with a product that suits you perfectly. And, of course, you won't be spending as much as you would if you bought your lip care products.

What You Need

The ingredients for homemade and natural lip care products are basically the same as those for making lotions and creams. Here are the most common and their functions.

Beeswax or Soywax	emollient; gives the desired hardness for easy handling
Shea Butter	moisturizing and anti-inflammatory
Cocoa Butter	emollient and antioxidant
Coconut oil	moisturizes, heals and protects
Vitamin E	antioxidant; prevents dryness
Essential Oils	give flavor and fragrance
Mica Powder or Beetroot powder	colorants

Storage

You can reuse lipstick or lip balm tubes or tins and 5 mL containers. Just be sure these have been thoroughly cleaned, sterilized, and dried. Most of the concoctions can be kept for at least a month in a cool, dry place. The harder the lip balm or Chapstick®, the longer it lasts. Some can even last for a year.

What to Watch out For

As usual, check for possible allergies before usage. Since you will be applying the concoctions on your lips, make sure ingredients are food grade, "pure" or "premium."

You may be sensitive to ingredients to plump the lips, like ginger or cinnamon oils and cayenne. Also, to best benefit from the moisturizing properties of the concoctions here, lips should be exfoliated with a mild scrub of sugar or salt with oil before application.

Adding water to the concoctions must be avoided as this could cause mold growth and spoilage.

Watch out for DIY lip balm kits that use substandard oils and include harmful dyes and other chemical ingredients. It's always best to handpick your own ingredients.

Lip Care Recipes

Honey-Coconut Healing Balm

Coconut oil and honey are both excellent moisturizers for the lips. They grab moisture from the air and keep it on the lips. Coconut oil also has antibacterial and antiviral properties that aid in healing, and it offers natural protection from the sun.

Makes: 1 ounce

Ingredients
1 tablespoon grated beeswax or beeswax pastilles
1 tablespoon virgin coconut oil
⅛ teaspoon honey
⅛ teaspoon vitamin E oil
10-15 drops of desired essential oil (try lavender, tea tree oil, or peppermint)

Directions
1. Melt the beeswax in a double boiler.
2. When about half of the beeswax has melted, add the coconut oil and honey.
3. Stir and continue heating until thoroughly melted.
4. Remove it from the heat.
5. Stir in the vitamin E oil and essential oils.
6. Pour the mixture into the prepared containers and let it cool.

Sugar Scrub

A simple scrub that's so simple and easy to make. Use this gentle exfoliant before applying lip balm for amazingly smooth, soft, and luscious lips.

Makes: 0.5 ounce

Ingredients
2 teaspoons granulated sugar or salt
1 teaspoon coconut or sunflower oil
½ teaspoon honey (optional)

Directions
1. Combine the ingredients.
2. Take a pinch of this mixture and rub it gently on your lips to remove rough, dead skin. You may also use a toothbrush to gently loosen dry layers.
3. Leave it on for about a minute, and then wipe it off.
4. Follow with lip balm.
5. Do this not more than twice a week.

Cinnamon Spice Lip Plumper

Get fuller, plumper, and sexier lips without expensive injections or surgery. The trick is to use mildly irritating ingredients that cause increased blood flow to the lips. The proportion of spices like cinnamon and cayenne causes very mild irritation but, because we all react differently, you'll have to experiment to determine how much will work best for you. This very mild recipe is a good beginner's concoction.

Makes: 0.13 -0.25 ounces

Ingredients
1 tube plain lip balm
½ teaspoon cinnamon oil or powder
¼ - ½ teaspoon cayenne powder, 35 K H.U. (optional)
3-5 drops vanilla flavor oil (optional)

Directions
1. Empty the contents of your lip balm tube (keep the tube for reuse) into a heatproof glass measuring cup or a mug.
2. Fill a small pot or saucepan with water to reach level with the contents of the cup. (Do not get any water into mixture!) and bring it to a simmer.
3. Immerse the measuring cup or mug with the balm in the simmering water (do not boil).
4. Stir, and allow the balm to melt.
5. Add the rest of the ingredients one by one, mixing well after each addition.
6. Transfer the mixture back into the original balm tube or into a container of your choice.

Balm & Tint

Soothing and moisturizing sweet almond and coconut oils, tinted with natural ingredients, will keep your lips looking moist with a hint of color.

Makes: 6 ounces

Ingredients
¼ cup beeswax
¼ cup sweet almond or coconut oil
¼ cup shea butter
Several drops pure essential oil of choice (such as rose, vanilla, or lavender)
1 teaspoon beetroot powder or cocoa powder (or a combination), for color

Directions
1. Put the beeswax in a heatproof glass measuring cup, or a mug.
2. Fill a small pot or saucepan with water to reach the level of the contents of the mug (Do not get any water into mixture!) and bring it to a simmer.
3. Immerse the measuring cup or mug with the balm in the simmering water (do not boil).
4. Stir and allow the beeswax to melt.
5. When half of the beeswax has melted, add the sweet almond oil and shea butter. Allow everything to melt.
6. Stir with a stainless steel spoon. To test for consistency, lift a small amount with the spoon and allow it to cool. Adjust the consistency by adding more beeswax (to thicken) or more oil (to thin), as needed.
7. Add the rest of the ingredients, mixing well after each addition. Make sure there are no lumps.
8. Pour into prepared containers.

Homemade Lipstick

The rich coconut oil and cocoa butter in this recipe keep your lips soft and hydrated in your own concocted color using mica powder. Mica powder is a safe and natural coloring agent that reflects light, making your lips look smooth and shimmery.

Serves: 4 ounces

Ingredients
3 tablespoons coconut oil
3 tablespoons cocoa butter
3 tablespoons beeswax
10 drops essential oil of choice (vanilla, grapefruit, rose, orange, etc.)
1 teaspoon mica powder (in a shade or combination of shades of your choice)

Directions
1. Melt the coconut oil, cocoa butter, and beeswax in a double boiler.
2. When fully melted, stir in the essential oils and mica powder. Mix well. Turn off the heat, but leave the mixture in the double boiler to keep it liquid.
3. To test the color and consistency, use a toothpick to pick up a small amount. Allow it to cool and test it on your lips. You may need to add a little more melted beeswax to make it harder, or more mica powder for more color.
4. Pour the mixture into prepared containers. If you are using tubes, use a pipette to transfer the mixture.
5. Allow the lipstick to cool before placing caps.

Basic Lip Balm

The best way to protect your lips from the harsh dry elements is to have a nourishing, moisturizing lip balm on hand.

Makes: 1.5 ounces

Ingredients
1 ½ tablespoons beeswax
2 tablespoons cocoa butter
2 tablespoons coconut oil
20 drops of essential oil of choice

Directions
1. Put the beeswax, cocoa butter, and coconut oil into a heatproof glass measuring cup or a mug.
2. Fill a small pot or saucepan with water to reach level of contents of cup or mug (Do not get any water into mixture!) and bring to a simmer.
3. When the contents have melted, turn off the heat but do not take the cup out of the hot water.
4. Stir in the essential oils.
5. Transfer the mixture into containers, or pipette into tubes.
6. Let it cool completely before capping.

Color and Plump Lipstick

A two-in-one lipstick that colors and gently plumps your lips. Its moisturizing ingredients ensure that your lips are always in great condition.

Makes: 4 ounces

Ingredients
3 tablespoons sweet almond oil
3 tablespoons cocoa butter
3 tablespoons beeswax
1 drop cinnamon oil
1 drop ginger oil
3-5 drops peppermint essential oil
1 drop clove oil (optional)
1 teaspoon mica powder (in a shade or combination of shades of your choice)

Directions
1. Melt the almond oil, cocoa butter, and beeswax in a double boiler.
2. When they are fully melted, stir in the essential oils and mica powder. Mix well. Turn off the heat, but leave the mixture in the double boiler to keep liquid.
3. To test the color and consistency, use a toothpick to pick up a small amount. Allow it to cool and test it on your lips. You may need to add a little more melted beeswax to make it harder, or more mica powder for more color.
4. Pour the mixture into prepared containers. If you are using tubes, use a pipette to transfer the mixture.
5. Allow it to cool before placing caps.
6. Apply to lips as you would lipstick. The plumping effect is mild and may not be immediately evident, as it is not meant to be wiped off like regular lip plumpers.

Sugar & Spice Lip Scrub & Plumper

Gently rub off dead layers while smoothing and plumping your lips.

Makes: 1 ½ ounces

Ingredients
1 tablespoon sunflower oil
1 teaspoon sugar
1 teaspoon cinnamon powder

Directions
1. Mix the ingredients together and keep them in a glass container.
2. To use, massage some on your lips and leave it on for 5-10 minutes.
3. Rinse off.

Hair Care

The hair should not be neglected when using natural, chemical-free products. Harmful chemicals from commercial products strip the hair and scalp of natural oils and leave buildup or residue that can cause damage and that may be absorbed into the body.

There are an abundance resources in nature that can maintain, enhance, or restore the health, shine, softness, and silkiness of our locks.

Benefits

Discover the many ingredients that are natural, safe, and gentle that can benefit your hair and scalp – ingredients that soothe itchiness, remove dandruff, restore natural oils, encourage hair growth, moisturize, soften, and so much more. All these at a very low cost compared to commercial products.

What You Need

The usual equipment in a regular kitchen is adequate for making homemade hair products. Most recipes are simple and very doable. For making hair care concoctions, a heatproof measuring cup, a blender or food processor, and a crockpot, double boiler, or microwave can come in handy.

Old shampoo or conditioner bottles can be cleaned and recycled. Glass jars or bottles are preferred by some because these are non-reactive and the concoctions are less likely to deteriorate too quickly.

Castile soap is a common base for homemade shampoos. It is non-toxic and does not strip the hair and scalp of natural oils.

Storage

Store homemade hair products in sterilized containers and refrigerate to preserve the quality. Shelf life can vary from a few days to a year; this all depends on factors such as water content, handling, and storage temperature.

What to Watch out For

One ingredient that many wish to avoid in commercial hair care products is sulfate. This is present in shampoos as sodium laureth sulfate, sodium lauryl sulfate, or ammonium laureth sulfate. A quick search on the internet will reveal several other ingredients containing sulfate. Sulfate is responsible for the foaming ability of your shampoos. It's what makes it possible for us to wash out the dirt from our hair. Unfortunately, the natural oils get washed out as well. Another reason for avoiding sulfate is that is aggravates scalp eczema. When using natural hair cleaners which are sulfate-free, your hair will never feel squeaky clean because the natural oils are retained.

We all react differently to different ingredients, and what works for your best friend may not work for you. Be open to the idea of experimenting with ingredients and their proportions to come up with the best formulation for you. Check for allergies before using any unfamiliar ingredients.

Hair Care Recipes

Hair Cream

Keep your tresses frizz-free, manageable and shiny with this cream. You can decide on which essential oils to use to create your very own scent.

Makes: 3 ounces

Ingredients
2 tablespoons shea butter
2 tablespoons coconut oil
1 teaspoon olive oil
1 teaspoon jojoba oil
¾ teaspoon sweet almond oil
1 tablespoon pure aloe vera gel
⅛ teaspoon vitamin E oil
15-20 drops essential oil of choice (like lavender or chamomile)

Directions
1. Melt the shea butter and coconut oil by placing them in a heatproof measuring cup over hot water in a pot or bowl. Do not let any water into the mixture.
2. Add the rest of the ingredients one by one, mixing well after each addition.
3. Pour the mixture into jar, shallow glass, or tin container and let it cool.
4. Refrigerate overnight.
5. Let it warm to room temperature for easy handling.
6. Rub a small amount in the palms of your hands and apply to dry or slightly damp hair.

Honey-Banana Hair Mask

Revive your hair with the super-moisturizing properties of bananas and honey. This hair mask is as good at conditioning your hair as it is to eat!

Serves:5 ounces

Ingredients
1 banana
1 tablespoon honey
2 tablespoons cream

Directions
1. Blend all the ingredients together. The banana should be thoroughly blended, with no bits or chunks, as these are difficult to rinse off.
2. Apply the conditioner to your hair and leave it on for about 10 minutes.
3. Rinse off with warm water.

Rinse for Shiny Hair

Apple cider vinegar removes buildup and restores softness and shine to hair. Rosemary stimulates hair growth and prevents graying. The tea of your choice adds fragrance.

Makes: 24 ounces

Ingredients
2 ½ cups hot water
½ cup apple cider vinegar
¼ sprig of rosemary
1 tea bag (flavor of choice)

Directions
1. Combine ingredients and let them sit for 30 minutes.
2. Dispense the liquid into a storage bottle, straining if needed. You may also use a spray bottle.
3. Shake before use. Apply or spray on hair.
4. Leave it on your hair for a minute or two, and then rinse it off.

Lemon-Cucumber Hair Detox

Let lemon cleanse your hair while cucumber conditions and refreshes. A simple way to detox your hair.

Makes: 8 ounces

Ingredients
1 lemon
1 cucumber
1 tablespoon olive or coconut oil
A few drops rosemary essential oil

Directions
1. Wash, peel, and slice the lemon and cucumber.
2. Combine all the ingredients and run them in a blender or food processor.
3. Strain, and pour it into a glass gar.
4. Massage into hair.
5. Rinse.
6. Refrigerate any leftovers for up to 10 days.

Anti-Dandruff Shampoo

Though not as foamy as commercial shampoos, this shampoo will keep your hair soft and clean. Your scalp will also benefit from the soothing and nourishing ingredients. Maintaining a magnificent mane has never been this easy and affordable!

Makes: 17 ounces

Ingredients
½ teaspoon jojoba oil
2 tablespoons liquid castile soap
⅔ cup herbal infusion (recipe below)

To make herbal infusion
1-2 teabags green tea
2 tablespoons burdock root
2 tablespoons chamomile
2 tablespoons rosemary
2 tablespoons fresh aloe vera gel OR a 2-3 inch piece of aloe vera stalk
2-3 cups distilled water
10 drops eucalyptus essential oil
10 drops lemon essential oil

Directions
To make the herbal infusion
1. Place the teabags and herbs in a small pot and add enough distilled water to cover the contents by 1 inch.
2. Bring it to a boil. Turn off the heat, cover, and let it sit for several hours or overnight.
3. Strain the mixture through cheesecloth and stir in the essential oils.
4. Keep refrigerated in a glass jar.

To make the shampoo

1. Combine all the ingredients in a glass or plastic bottle.
2. Shake well and use as regular shampoo.

Green Tea Shampoo

Green tea does wonders for the hair as it fights off radicals, inflammation, and hair loss. It helps restore hair's luster while encouraging hair growth. Surprisingly, achieving thick, silky and shiny hair can be this easy!

Makes: 9 ounces

Ingredients
1-2 teabags green tea
1 cup pure liquid castile soap
1 tablespoon olive oil
1 teaspoon honey

Directions
1. Steep the tea bags in freshly boiled water for 30 minutes. Drain and let it cool to room temperature.
2. Combine all the ingredients and use as any regular shampoo.

Beer & Vinegar Rinse

This easy-to-make hair rinse will revive and condition you hair, restoring bounce and luster.

Makes: 8 ounces

Ingredients
½ cup beer
½ cup apple cider vinegar

Directions
1. Apply on the hair and leave on for not more than 5 minutes.
2. Rinse off.

Anti-Baldness Hair Treatment

Lemon conditions the scalp and hair to fight off itchiness and flakes. Aloe vera induces thick and healthy hair growth.

Makes: 2 ounces

Ingredients
1 tablespoon fresh lemon juice
3 tablespoons aloe vera gel
½ teaspoon olive oil (optional)

Directions
1. Mix the ingredients together.
2. Apply and massage into the scalp.
3. Leave it on for 15 minutes, then rinse it off.
4. Follow with a gentle shampoo.
5. Repeat three times a week.

Hair Growth & Anti-Baldness Paste

The enzymes in aloe vera make the scalp conditions ideal for hair growth. Aloe vera has been known for centuries as a natural hair-growth inducer. It also has anti-dandruff and anti-itching properties. It conditions and detangles hair, giving you soft, lustrous locks. Fenugreek and basil have been recognized in Ayurvedic medicine as effective in inducing hair growth and preventing baldness.

Makes: 6 ounces

Ingredients
½ cup fresh aloe vera gel
2 teaspoons castor oil
2 teaspoons fenugreek powder
1 teaspoon basil powder
Distilled water

Directions
1. Combine all the ingredients, gradually adding just enough distilled water to form a paste.
2. Massage the paste into the scalp. Cover with a towel or shower cap and leave it on for 10 minutes. Better still, leave it on for several hours or overnight once or twice a week.
3. Rinse off and follow with a gentle shampoo.

Hair Gel

A hair gel that's easy to make and inexpensive, without any harmful preservatives or alcohol. You can choose the essential oils you want to make your own scent.

Makes: 4 ounces

Ingredients
¼ teaspoon unflavored gelatin powder
½ cup hot distilled water
4-6 drops essential oil of choice

Directions
1. Mix the gelatin in hot water and stir to dissolve.
2. Cool and refrigerate until it is set.
3. Stir in the essential oils.
4. Transfer to a desired container. (You can reuse cleaned empty hair gel bottles).
5. Keeps in the refrigerator for 2 weeks.

Men's Care

Men are also bombarded with the damaging chemicals in their own grooming aids. This is aside from the beating their skin can get from the elements. The recipes here are especially formulated for the man of today who values his health as well as his looks.

Benefits

It is always well worth the extra effort to create grooming aids that contain natural, safe, and gentle ingredients that condition hair and skin just as well, in fact better, than what we spend so much on at the store. There is also the added enjoyment and reward in being able to make personal products customized according to one's own requirements.

What You Need

The principles and ingredients for making products for men and for women do not differ very much. Scents that are more appealing to males can be achieved by using the right combination of essential oils. Some scents that are more popular with men are those of cedar, oak moss, myrrh, lime, sandalwood, cypress, and bergamot. There are several scents to choose from and combine to make a scent to suit a man's taste perfectly.

Storage

Basically, using a sterilized, non-reactive container for your concoctions will help them keep longer. The shelf life can vary depending on many factors like water content, exposure to light or heat, and contamination from handling. Discard anything that begins to smell or look odd.

What to Watch out For

A man's skin can be just as sensitive as a woman's, so be sure to check for sensitivity to unfamiliar ingredients before use.

Men's Care Recipes

Aftershave Spritz

Witch hazel is an excellent aftershave as it soothes the skin and acts as an antiseptic and astringent. Vegetable glycerin keeps your skin moist. You may make your own combination of essential oils to create your own unique scent.

Makes: 8 ounces

Ingredients
1 cup witch hazel (liquid)
1 teaspoon vegetable glycerin
6 drops sweet orange oil
3 drops sandalwood or peppermint essential oil

Directions
1. Combine all the ingredients in a spray bottle and shake well.
2. Spritz or splash on the face after shaving.

Aftershave Cream

This one is specifically for the men out there, as it makes an excellent after-shave cream. It helps to soothe irritated and inflamed skin. Tea tree oil has anti-fungal and anti-bacterial properties. The coconut oil and shea butter will deeply nourish your skin.

Makes: 30 ounces.

Ingredients
1 ⅛ cup cocoa butter
1 ½ cups coconut oil
6 tablespoons jojoba oil
40 drops tea tree oil
50 drops lavender essential oil or any essential oil of your choice

Directions
1. Place the cocoa butter in a bowl. Place the bowl over a saucepan with simmering water. When it is melted, remove it from the heat.
2. Add the coconut oil, jojoba oil, and lavender essential oil. Stir well.
3. Place the mixture in the refrigerator for a while.
4. When the oil mixture begins to solidify slightly, whip it with a whisk until you get a buttery and creamy consistency. You can also put it in a blender and blend on high speed, pulsing every 10 seconds until the mixture becomes light and fluffy.
5. Add the tea tree oil once you are done with the whipping.
6. Spoon it into a glass jar. Cover the mixture with a tight lid.
7. Store in a cool and dry place.

Basic Aftershave Cream & Moisturizer

The moisturizing ingredients in this cream help give you a smoother, hassle-free shave.

Makes: 5 ounces

Ingredients
⅛ cup coconut oil
½ cup shea butter
4 drops of essential oil of choice (like lavender or chamomile)

Directions
1. Melt the shea butter by putting it in a heatproof measuring cup placed over hot water.
2. Transfer the softened shea butter to a blender, and add the rest of the ingredients.
3. Run until creamy in consistency.
4. Keep refrigerated.
5. Apply a thin layer to skin after shaving.

Cool-As-A-Cucumber Windburn Balm

Chamomile is effective for soothing burns and inflammation in skin. Mixed with cooling cucumber, your skin will quickly lose the sting of wind- and sunburns. The essential oils should be sparing and not warming. Healing essential oils are lavender and bergamot.

Makes: 8 ounces

Ingredients
¼ cup boiling water
2 bags chamomile tea
1 whole cucumber, unpeeled and chopped
¼ cup aloe vera gel
2 drops lavender or bergamot essential oil

Directions
1. Steep the tea bags in the hot water until they have cooled to room temperature.
2. Remove the tea bags, squeezing out as much liquid as possible. Discard the tea bags.
3. Place all ingredients together in a blender and run until a smooth cream is formed.
4. Strain out any bits, if needed.
5. Refrigerate to cool.
6. Apply to affected areas and leave it on for 15 minutes.
7. Rinse off with cool water, and apply moisturizer.

Lemony Foaming Facial Wash

A facial wash which mildly exfoliates, cleanses, and lightens. This helps you start the day feeling refreshed and confident.

Makes: 8 ounces

Ingredients
1 cup natural sugar
½ teaspoon white rice powder
½ teaspoon calendula powder
½ teaspoon chamomile powder
½ teaspoon lavender powder
⅛ teaspoon orange peel powder
6 teaspoons castile soap, pure, unscented
½ teaspoon lemongrass essential oil

Directions
1. In a bowl, combine the sugar with the powders. Mix well.
2. Add the castile soap and mix well.
3. Lastly, add the essential oil and mix thoroughly.
4. Transfer to prepared containers.
5. Take about half a teaspoon of the mixture and rub between damp hands.
6. Apply it on the face in a circular motion.
7. Rinse off.
8. Gently dry skin and follow with moisturizer.

Acne-Fighting Cleanser

Activated charcoal and tea tree oil in an ultra-mild soap help to clear up skin and fight bacteria that aggravate acne. The herbal as well as rice powders help to soothe, nourish, and prevent further breakouts.

Makes: 8 ounces

Ingredients
1 cup natural sugar
¼ teaspoon activated charcoal
½ teaspoon white rice powder
½ teaspoon calendula powder
½ teaspoon chamomile powder
½ teaspoon lavender powder
6 teaspoons castile soap, pure, unscented
½ teaspoon lemongrass essential oil
10 drops tea tree oil

Directions
1. In a bowl, combine the sugar with the powders. Mix well.
2. Add the castile soap and mix well.
3. Lastly, add the essential oils and mix thoroughly.
4. Transfer to prepared containers.
5. Take about half a teaspoon of the mixture and rub between damp hands.
6. Apply it on the face in a circular motion.
7. Rinse off.
8. Gently dry skin and follow with moisturizer.

Soothing and Moisturizing Cream

This cream is packed with moisturizing and nourishing ingredients. Coconut oil moisturizes without suffocating the skin, while also protecting against bacteria and viruses. Tea tree oil is mildly antiseptic and effective against acne. Vetiver, though not very well known, has amazing anti-aging properties and a very pleasant aroma.

Makes: 7 ounces

Ingredients
⅓ cup shea butter
⅓ cup virgin coconut oil
¼ cup almond oil
5-7 drops vetiver essential oil
10-15 drops tea tree oil

Directions
1. Soften the shea butter in a double boiler, or in a heatproof cup over a pot of hot water.
2. Once softened, add the rest of the ingredients and mix thoroughly.
3. Cover and refrigerate until the mixture has solidified.
4. Whip with a hand mixer until a fluffy cream is formed.
5. Pour into prepared jars. Keep it refrigerated while unused.
6. Rub a small amount in damp hands and gently apply to the face in a circular motion.
7. Rinse off, pat dry, and follow with a gentle moisturizer.

Blackhead Remover

This combination of ingredients you probably have on hand gently but expertly unclogs pores, while conditioning and lightening the skin.

Makes: 2 ½ ounces

Ingredients
2 tablespoons oatmeal
3 tablespoons yogurt
½ teaspoon lemon juice
¼ teaspoon olive oil

Directions
1. Combine the ingredients to make a paste.
2. Apply on the face, spreading as evenly as possible, but not too close to the eyes.
3. Leave it on for a few minutes. You will feel the paste begin to dry and tighten a little.
4. Rinse off.

Pomade

Get that sleek, well-groomed look with this nourishing pomade with the scent that you prefer.

Makes: 6 ounces

Ingredients
3 tablespoons beeswax
3 tablespoons coconut oil
3 drops essential oil of choice

Directions
1. Melt the beeswax in a double boiler.
2. Once melted, add the rest of the ingredients and stir well.
3. Transfer to a tin or jar and allow it to cool until set.
4. Rub a pea-sized amount in the hands and apply to hair.

Beard Balm

Beards are becoming popular again and you'll need some help from this handy balm to keep looking dapper.

Makes: 3 ounces

Ingredients
2 tablespoons grated or chopped beeswax or beeswax pastilles
2 tablespoons shea butter
1 tablespoon cocoa butter
3 teaspoons jojoba oil
2 teaspoons sweet almond oil
3 drops lime essential oil
4-8 drops cedar essential oil
1 drop rosemary essential oil

Directions
1. Soften the beeswax in a double boiler.
2. When it is almost melted, add the rest of the ingredients EXCEPT the essential oils.
3. When the mixture is fully melted, stir in the essential oils a little at a time until you achieve the desired scent.
4. Pour it into containers and allow it to cool.
5. Rub a tiny amount between your hands and apply it on your beard.

Deodorant

The safe and mild yet effective ingredients that make up this homemade deodorant will keep you smelling clean while you sweat naturally. Odor and moisture are kept under control, while coconut and tea tree oils keep bacteria in check. This recipe ensures that the deodorant stick doesn't melt even in hot weather.

Makes: 6 ounces

Ingredients
1 tablespoon grated beeswax
3 tablespoons coconut oil
¼ cup corn starch
¼ cup baking soda
5 drops tea tree oil
5 drops of sandalwood or bergamot essential oil

Directions
1. Soften the beeswax in a double boiler.
2. Add the coconut oil and let it melt until it is completely liquid.
3. Stir in the remaining ingredients until you reach the consistency of a thin paste.
4. Work quickly, as the mixture will solidify fast.
5. Pour the deodorant into empty deodorant stick containers (commercial ones can be reused).
6. Allow them to harden.

Conclusion

You get one body in this lifetime and that body is covered with one of your hardest-working organs, your skin! Your skin is a shield from the elements and regulates what your body takes in from the environment. Much of the pollution in the air consists of particles we can't see, but that our skin blocks for us. With your skin doing all this heavy lifting, it is absolutely essential you give it the right nourishment to maintain its function.

Body scrubs help get rid of skin that is dead and in turn reveal the plump, soft, baby skin underneath. Lotions and butters help to pull moisture in, which is absolutely essential for youthful, glowing skin. Butters help to create a nice, thick, protective layer to retain moisture that is going to ensure your shield, aka your skin, is in top form.

The ease of creating skincare products at home will make you an absolute believer that homemade is best. Beyond the ease is that fact that the recipes included in this book are clean and natural. You can feel really good about what you are putting on and into your body. Your skin will thank you for it!

Enjoy that glow!

More Books from Josephine Simon

Made in the USA
Columbia, SC
10 March 2020